# Global Epidemic
## The Fear That Cripples
### by
### Dr. Mark Taylor

Born in 1962 in Macon, Georgia, Dr Mark Taylor expressed a keen interest in human behavior and cognitive development since an early age. This led him to pursue B.Min and M.Min degrees in Ministry/Counseling, followed by a Ph. D. in Cognitive Studies. Dr. Taylor served in the United States Air Force for 9 years, and is a Gulf War Veteran. He has offered various counseling services which required in depth analysis and reporting. Dr. Mark Taylor also holds a B.S. in Business Administration/Economics and a Doctorate of Divinity degree and is licensed for ministerial counseling. The potential societal benefits that can be derived from the application of such wealth of experience and education motivated Dr Taylor to dedicate himself to the dissipation of essential knowledge, applicable to the average citizen. He is the founder of USA180, one of the fastest growing 527 political organization in the U.S.

Dr. Taylor recently stepped down as National Director of USA180 to focus more on several ongoing projects pertaining to alternative energy, programs to aid G.E.D completion, programs to promote effective family financial planning as well as efficient housing, and medical research in the areas of cancer and autoimmune diseases.

Dr. Taylor owned and operated an Atlanta, Georgia based Consulting/Construction business for nearly 15 years. During this time He donated his time weekly to the Court systems. Working with individuals with difficulties in the drug courts and criminal court. There was always an opening in his company for individuals that had a desire to turn their lives around. Dr. Taylor not only made his expertise available to the courts, but to any person that had a desire to turn their life around. Dr. Taylor often said "If all my efforts only ever aided or helped just one life then all was worth it".

Dr. Taylor is currently forming a foundation (EarthOne) that will bring all of the projects he is involved with under one roof. Every project has one common thread, they are much needed in our society both U.S. and abroad. Dr. Taylor is working with Individuals from the United States, and the United Kingdom. EarthOne has many projects planned. Many open to the public. Visit EarthOne website to stay up to date on current projects, and future books. There will be sections of EarthOne that will need volunteers at all levels. Get involved. Contact EarthOne if you feel you would like to volunteer or establish a local group to make available in your area plans, and projects Earthone will be offering. Contact Dr. Taylor Eartone.Books@gmail.com  or visit Earthone website www.earthone-books.com  (Site will be up soon).

# Table of Contents

# Forward

## By Raymond John Francis Moore, Ph. D.

## Historian,United Kingdom

As the Dylan song says "Times They Are A Changing" There's a new American president, the world economy is crashing, job losses by the tens of thousands and predicted to get worse, foreclosures mounting exponentially both sides of the Atlantic, rumours of wars and food shortages and the list could go on. So if Barrack Obama does give hope to many across the planet and not only America, stressful times are still on us aplenty. There can be no doubt that this depression, and it is a depression, will only deepen. And therein lies a whole psychological process which includes not only stress but fear, worry, anxiety, feelings of panic and all the related illnesses this will cause. Not a time to bury one's head in the sand. Time to embrace it and tackle it head on. I think most people wish for a quick fix. All this will do is lengthen your wish list. Only unlike your Christmas card list you can't strike off anything or anyone should they offend, disturb, frighten or perplex you beyond what you would normally expect throughout a normal daily life or routine. This will happen. Face it and grab it by the horns before the horns pierce and have you flailing about in a wilderness of despair. Do it for yourself and most of all for those around you.

These are times many people will be searching desperately for someone of strength and fortitude. You can achieve this by following the excellent and tried advice by Dr. Taylor in this book. Dr. Taylor was once a resident of our Great Country. A welcome guest indeed. You owe it to yourself and all your fellow man whether they be perceived enemies or your closest friend to read this book. Good luck and good guidance.

*******

*Dr. Moore, a great friend and colleague has given me the honor and privilege of co-authoring a book along with him that will be released soon. To get on the information list. Email: earthone.books@gmail.com website www.earthone-books.com*

Warmest Regards,
Dr. Mark Taylor

# Introduction

Multi-tasking has become the norm in our society. A norm that has permeated the private sector and no longer is it strictly a corporate term. Has it been disastrously convoluted with an old adage - "can't walk and chew gum at the same time", making the inability for some to accomplish this feat a negative or an indication of ones inability to adapt to current trends? Has this placed an invisible benchmark that some cannot achieve? The modern term "multi-tasking" derives its meaning from the computer industries known phrase "multi-tasking" which refers to multiple computer functions working simultaneously.

In the mid to late eighties there were many buzz words coined. Many of these words seem to have come on the scene as desktop computers were evolving, and at a time of significant awareness of wasteful spending in the government, and private sector. There was much debate over balanced budgets in Washington. The Gramm/Rutman legislation was much debated. Emphasis was placed on negligent spending and more efficient allocation of resources , both human resources as well as non-human resources.

In the mix of things that transpired over the last two decades we can extract words like Synergy, Multitasking,etc..... Each of these came about over a two decade period, and all of these new terms or philosophies are to lead to more efficient spending and allocation of resources, both in the form of personnel, and non-human resources.

One critical factor was left out, the human factor. I lend this to the influence of the minds that have brought about our dependence on computer technology. While these advances have had a tremendous positive impact on our society I feel there are multiple repercussions that are certainly negative and adversely impacting our society.

The fact that we are human and not computers is where my contention can be found. This convolution of computers and humans has had a devastating impact on our psychological well being. While a computer can handle multi-tasking with impunity the human being can only sustain this to a certain level or for a certain time period before displaying signs of psychological distress.

Multitasking is considered in some camps as necessary for proper time management not only in the work place, but also at home. Yet when we consider a simple scenario like the dangers of talking on your cell phone and driving at the same time I find it prudent to consider the adverse effects in a much broader scope. Scientifically speaking this simple example demands us to take a closer look into the overall implications.

# The Art Of Multi-Tasking

One formal meaning of multitasking is "the concurrent performance of several jobs by computer."Over time, the term has changed into something far from its original meaning,and it is now in common practice applied to people in the work place as well. Author Alison Overholt asks, "How do you stay sane when you are insanely busy? You become very good at multitasking."

Today's society seems to accept this idea of multi-tasking as being normal. Not only normal but in many or rather most cases absolutely essential to our success as a business person in the 21st century . Author Ellen Ullman states in an Op-Ed piece to the New York Times, this skill (multi-tasking) "has become the hallmark of a successful citizen of the 21st century."

While the ability or expected ability to multi-task is beneficial, leading experts are finding it has equally many adverse effects, and pitfalls as well. Human beings simply are not machines, and it is judicious to proceed with caution considering these are areas that have never been explored, but are at the same time being imposed on society.

Is it any wonder that everywhere we turn we are hearing the words "I'm so stressed out"? People are experiencing pressure as never before, and it is causing stress as never before. Many are finding that they are ill equipped to deal with these stressors that often trigger anxiety and other symptoms which can and often do make us sick. Literally, sick.

The numbers are overwhelming, shocking even. Roughly one in eight Americans between the age of 18 and 54 suffers from stress/anxiety disorders. These numbers are pre-financial bailout figures. I am certain that these numbers are much higher, and will climb higher as the economy tightens.

It is shown that females suffer from anxiety or stress related issues, and disorders twice as much as males. Anxiety has become the most common mental illness in the United States. Anxiety has easily moved well ahead of depression. In more cases than not anxiety is a precursor to depression.

Anxiety is now the most commonly reported mental health issues affecting adults over the age of 64. Anxiety, and Stress related disorders now cost the United States in excess of 47 billion per year as of 2007. This number will increase or has already.

The average person suffering from anxiety typically sees a doctor or doctors 5 times on average before receiving a diagnosis. This is due to the varied symptoms produced, and the fact that most wait until physical symptoms occur before seeking help.

Stress and anxiety come as a duo, hand in hand. The leading symptom of stress is anxiety. Amazingly stress accounts for 75 to 85 percent of all illnesses either directly or indirectly. Stress is far more dangerous than we had imagined. Stress adversely affects blood pressure and can if not treated highly increase chances of stroke. Recent health insurance companies have reported that 90 percent of visits to a primary care physician were stress related.

Studies have revealed that prolonged stress directly affects the body's immune system making a person suffering from stress more susceptible to diseases. They are also more susceptible to allergic reactions, and cardiovascular, and autoimmune diseases.

Doctors agree that chronic stress can cause non-essential body functions to shut down. Functions like the digestive and immune systems which in turn makes the person sick. In many instances psychosomatic illnesses occur. This is an illness with an emotional and or psychological element.

In an attempt to alleviate or self medicate many people resort to heavy smoking, drinking, and drugs. Many develop poor eating habits and become totally inactive further causing their health to deteriorate.

Stress is a part of life. We need to be aware of the fact that the way we react to this stress is what determines the impact to our health. We will never be able to completely eliminate stress from our lives, but we can learn healthy methods of dealing with it, greatly reducing negative impact to our personal health.

It would seem that we could in some way avoid stress in life, but I have found it nearly impossible. At best we can reduce our stress, by eliminating what we can control, and learning to deal

with what we have no control over in a healthy manner.
One of the greatest things we can learn in life is the fact that we cannot effectively control people, places or things. We can only effectively control ourselves, and many find this achievable task daunting. Yet many continue to try and change other people, and their behaviors.

Having a great deal of experience in the addiction field I found this very thing (controlling others) to be one of the major obstacles in recovery. If one has difficulty accepting this fact, they have little chance of recovery. It has even become part of a prayer which is commonly recited in the twelve step programs of Alcoholics Anonymous and Narcotics Anonymous.

*God grant me the serenity to accept the things I cannot change; courage to change the things I can; and wisdom to know the difference.*

I decided after the economic problems escalated to a point that all were aware of it that I would write this book so that the average person could understand stress, and anxiety. My studies in Christian counseling, and Cognitive Studies coupled with the fact that I myself suffered from anxiety at one point could help someone identify early on a sometimes hard to diagnose problem. The earlier we can catch this, the better off we are as with any other disorder. The problem with anxiety or stress related issues is the ability of it to manifest its self in other physiological disorders.

I was in my mid thirties and had left the counseling field in the boom times of the 90's in Atlanta to run my own construction/consulting business. During this time if you owned a construction business you "were in the money". Atlanta experienced tremendous growth throughout the 90's.

This I found to be rather interesting. I had gone to lunch with a paint supplier. A Sherwin Williams representative to be exact. We dined at a local Mexican restaurant. As we left, my supplier was paying the tab at which point I noticed a stiffness in my chest. At first I thought it to be a case of heart burn coming on.

I had, due to my poor eating habits, eating on the go,etc., frequent bouts of heartburn. So I paid it little attention. Upon getting in the vehicle it got worse. I experienced a racing heartbeat. It was quite different from any other instance of heart burn. This of course caused me some concern. Alarm would be more appropriate. This simply added to the problem. It was apparent I was in distress, because my guest noticed and asked if I was okay. Of course I played it off and got him back to his office as quickly as possible.

After delivering my rep. back to his office I pulled over and relaxed in the parking lot. I still felt very odd. I decided that I should go to the doctor. I turned onto the street and went roughly two blocks and it hit again. My chest tightened and this time it scared me. I felt light headed and due to the fear I experienced my breathing became labored. I had no clue I was experiencing a panic or anxiety attack. I did however, think at the time I was having a heart attack!

Anxiety was the last thing on my mind. After all this was boom time and money was great. I had no care in the world, I thought. I was extremely busy, and worked insane hours. I also had awful eating habits, not to mention terrible sleep habits. I was a prime target. Stress is stress, and does not always take on a negative form. The lifestyle I had built oozed of stress. Due to my awful life style habits i.e. Eating, and sleeping habits, stress took its toll and manifested in the form of an anxiety attack.

This truly scared me and I immediately decided to go directly to an emergency room instead of my doctor. It seemed to take forever but finally I wheeled into the Atlanta Veterans Hospital. I am a United States Air Force Gulf War Veteran so I knew they would see me with no hassle. It was a couple minutes extra to go there, but I knew they had one of the best trauma centers in Atlanta. I arrived and was seen instantly. Chest pains should never be taken lightly. You should never take chest pains lightly, NEVER! I was given aspirin to chew immediately. This is done to thin the blood in the event of a heart attack or if I was actually, presently having one. Aspirin can save your life if taken at the onset of a heart attack. I was given a cardiogram, and subjected to various blood tests. I spent roughly six hours there. They actually wanted me to stay overnight. I of course refused now feeling much better. All the tests came back fine. They scheduled me for stress tests in which I would come back later and take and pass with flying colors. Final diagnosis, Anxiety attack. What!

Yes anxiety attack Dr. Taylor. Yes they put much emphasis on doctor as if I should have known better. I am no M.D. simply a counselor, a Christian counselor to be exact. I knew I truly had to change my habits (both eating and sleeping). I did manage to sort things out to a point that I no longer suffered from these attacks. After the first one I knew what they were so I would just make myself relax, and soon they would pass. Not something you want to deal with for long periods, because they can seem like a heart attack, and one never knows if they may be ignoring a real heart attack thinking it is just an anxiety attack. Furthermore, stress not dealt with can and will cause physiological problems. It could be in the form of lowering ones immune system making you susceptible to many diseases or manifest into a cardiovascular disorder.

What I would like to outline in the forthcoming pages are ways to cope with this potentially debilitating disorder. Certainly there are many drugs on the market that allow a person to tolerate exposure to high levels of stress, but could this possibly be healthy? Should we immediately be placed on medication before exhausting natural methods of coping or eliminating stress? I feel that every avenue should be explored before resorting to psychotropics (mood altering drugs). Many of these drugs hit the market and can have adverse effects.

## So Why Are We So Stressed Out

This world is off the hook. It is getting crazier by the day. We constantly tell ourselves it will get better, but we awaken each day to face more and more absurdities. Nothing seems safe anymore. Our jobs are at risk. Our homes are at risk as America experiences historically record breaking foreclosures. 1 in 8 homes are either in foreclosure or at least 2 to 3 payments behind. Unemployment is at an all time high yet our politicians continue to tell us everything is fine when we know damn well everything is not. Then finally they admit it right before a record bailout is catered in.

Now the apathetic majority of America has been shaken from it's slumber to only add to the problem. Griping and moaning over a problem that perhaps had they been awake and acting as responsible citizens, we may not be experiencing.

Then we have the "freedom movement". Last time I checked we were free. If you allow yourself to be subjected to an over abundance of this lot you will have stress related issues. You will hear a wide variety of reasons for our current problems. You have your impeachment crowd, the end the Federal Reserve crowd and the Alien crowd. In addition, the New World Order Theories are out of control. There is so much paranoia in this bunch that it's scary.

I have been called a reptilian, a disinformation specialist and the list goes on. The paranoia is so high that most of the personal attacks on me came from supposed fellow patriots.

Do not mistake me as I support any organization or person that is set out to preserve or better our country. It is those that exaggerate the issues or add their own made up additions that I am referring to, and there are quite a few that fit this description. It truly is off the hook. One thing that is lacking in this whole scenario is the "Fix The Citizen Crowd".

Much of our problems can be traced to our lack of involvement, and the fact that we have become nothing more than materialistic consumer gluttons, and allowed things to get out of control, and now we want to point fingers. We must first look in the mirror. If we fail to do this we are exerting energy, and pointing fingers hoping for a solution in total and absolute vain. That is however, another story.

*Did you know that when you are pointing a finger, there are always three fingers pointing back?? Do it now. Point and look at your hand!*

As you can see we truly live in a hectic society mostly created by our own design. I fear it is going to get worse before we see things take a turn for the better. So we had better learn, and learn in a fast manner how to cope, how to deal with this thing called stress in a healthy fashion.

We have truly entered into the "Age of Anxiety". Time Magazine carried a story in 2002 dealing with this topic. I do not think the author knew how accurate he was, nor how bad it would get. Yes we are in the "Age of Anxiety". "Yes We Can" adapt, and deal with it. I truly hope President Obama stands true to his word, and brings about a positive, healthy change that is well over due in America. The kind of change that will reshape our image in the eyes of the world, and restore our dignity as the leading Nation that stands for Rights, Liberties and Freedom. Never have I seen a need to give up freedom to maintain freedom nor have you. "Yes We Can" We can only pray. We are counting on you Barack Obama.

*The stress in our country has grown to the point that our children feel it. Ask them. They know something is not right. Our stress as adults certainly has and will spill over on to our children.*

## Common Behaviors That May Feed Stress

There are three major behaviors that are often overlooked. A couple of these may be good traits in moderation but if overly used, will feed to your stress.

One is **obsessive negativity**. Being obsessively negative is indicative of a negative outlook on your life, toward people, places, and things in your life.
Do you find yourself constantly saying things like "I can't do this" or "no one understands"?

This is an easy ditch to get in, especially in today's environment. The economy is bad and getting worse. Unemployment is at a historical high, and home foreclosures are setting record highs. Unfortunately this will get worse before it gets better so it would be prudent to view life through a positive lens as

I have learned to do. We have to learn to play the cards that are dealt. We have to be able to recognize the things we can change and act on them, and let those things go that we have no control over.

Acceptance plays a major role. Our ability to accept the things we cannot change will certainly lighten our stress load. We can strip ourselves of impossible tasks. Accepting a given situation does not necessitate having to like it. You do however, in order to remain mentally healthy, need to be able to accept those things we have no control over and move on. Also the items we can change we must do so without delay. Otherwise we allow problems to build up until they will finally manifest in some form of stress.

**Obsessive Perfection**. Yes this may sound bizarre yet I know you have run across this behavior if not being guilty of displaying it yourself at some point in time. There is nothing wrong with wanting to perform or do a task to the best of your ability. I am talking about obsessing over tasks to the point of being uptight. To the point of feeling nothing is ever good enough. Thinking if it is not accomplished to perfection others will view you as a failure. Be careful not to be overly concerned to the point of becoming an uptight jerk. You know the type. This is an annoying trait to have to deal with in a person. Enough said on this item. You know the type. Don't do it. It will eventually pile up to the point that it will manifest itself in an undesirable manner.

Lastly we have **Obsessive Analysis**. This comes with overly analyzing and feeling that it has to be mastered or figured out. You find this a lot in the Technology field. It is not an insult, but simply the way they train their brains to think. I use them as an example only because many in the I.T. world do this, and it is just the best analogy I can come up with. They spend countless hours working with code and trying to figure out sequences of code that will achieve their goal. Now take this same person out and ask them to fix a PC. Sometimes you will see these knowledgeable folks dissecting the issue when there is a simple fix. I have encountered situations where it appeared the engineer was going to dismantle the system. Why? Because they have trained themselves to understand each detail, and feel that to properly fix the instrument they have to take it apart, and more importantly to fully understand the problem. Not just fix it , but to know why it came to be a problem as well.

Maybe a poor example but one that comes to mind. If repeated in many areas of your life it can easily lead to a feeling of never completely doing anything to its fullest which in turn will build tremendous stress.

*If you feel you are allowing these behaviors you can alter them. If you are not sure whether you are falling victim to these stressful behaviors ask a close friend or loved one, but be willing to hear things that may upset you. Take it for what it is, and that is to gather helpful information. You may also want to keep a journal. Many dislike writing, but if you do it properly you will soon see patterns develop that will allow you to see the situations that cause these behaviors.*

## Stress Or Anxiety

Our society has grown accustom to using anxiety and stress synonymously. Yet there is a distinct difference between the two. Stress comes from pressures we feel from over expectations in the workplace and other situations that place us under a great deal of strain and pressure. It could be an over bearing spouse or an unruly child. In today's environment it can come from increasing unemployment, and the constantly rising cost of living. Not knowing if we will have a job tomorrow certainly produces stress. The discomfort we feel from these types of situations and many more can be labeled as stress or stressors.

Stress results in the release of adrenaline; a hormone. When this hormone (adrenaline) is present in high levels it will in most cases cause a rise in blood pressure, and many other negative physical symptoms. It is so very important for those that suffer from hypertension to avoid stressors as best possible.

Anxiety is one of the many negative and most common effects of stress. When one is stricken with anxiety fear overcomes all emotions. The victim tends to worry over everything often making the person a recluse and what is often referred to as a basket of nerves. You often hear it called the jitters. More severe symptoms are chest pains, dizziness, and shortness of breath. Then we have the most dreaded, the anxiety or panic attack.

As stated, stress is caused by situations that place you under pressure (tolerance levels vary from person to person) referred to as stressors. What may be a stressor to one person may not phase the next person. There are a countless number of things that would qualify as a stressor, depending on the individual. Stress can derive from things that make you angry, frustrated, and believe it or not being overly bored. Anxiety on the other hand is stress that remains after the stressor is gone or the situation causing the pressure is gone.

Anxiety is a feeling of fear, apprehension, and in almost all cause accompanies feelings of impending doom or the feeling that something dreadful is about to happen. The source of these feelings of uneasiness is not always known which simply adds to the discomfort.

We all experience stress at some time and to some degree. Stress is our body's way of reacting to things that disturb the normal balance in our lives. A very good example of this would be when we become frightened or find ourselves in a dangerous perhaps life threatening situation. Our adrenal glands then release the adrenaline hormone which activates our body's natural defense mechanisms causing our muscles to tense, and our blood pressure to rise. You will see a dilation of the pupils in the eyes.

This defense mechanism has enabled people to do super human things at times. There have been stories of where a woman lifting a car by the bumper to release a child that had been trapped underneath. Stress is a natural and sometimes life saving reaction. It is the constant stress or the stress that is far too frequent that causes the problems.

A good indication of increased stress is a rise in your pulse rate; however, a normal pulse rate does not always mean you are not stressed. Constant aches and pains, anxiety, heart palpitations, constant fatigue, crying, over eating or not eating enough, frequent infections, and even a decrease in your sexual desire are signs that may be noticed which indicate that you may be under stress or as it is said, "stressed out".

Every time we are under stress, we do not react to such an extreme and we are not always under such great duress or fear every time we are confronted with a stressful situation.

Some people are more susceptible than others to stress as I mentioned before; for some, even ordinary daily decisions seem insurmountable. Deciding what to have for dinner or what to buy at the store, is a seemingly, monumental problem for them. On the other hand, there are those people, who seem to thrive under stress by becoming highly productive being driven by the force of pressure. I personally operate, and produce far more under stress. I have learned to adjust this in myself due to the aforementioned anxiety attack, and the fact that I do personally have a history of hypertension which is under control by way of diet, fitness, and medication. The fitness or physical exercise is also great for stress.

Research shows women with children have higher levels of stress related hormones in their blood than women without children. Does this mean women without children do not experience stress? No!

It means that women without children usually are not subjected to as many stressful situations, and those with children have abundant opportunities to experience situations that can prove to be quite stressful. It is very important for mothers or parents in general to schedule time for themselves so that they are better equipped in times of stress, and it is also very important to exercise.

I cannot stress the importance of exercise enough. It does not have to be anything complicated. Many set up exercise programs that are impossible to maintain. Taking walks or running is fine. Weight Lifting is fine for those that are into that, but be careful that you include a good amount of cardiovascular in your exercise routine.

Cardiovascular is the most important. Always consult your family physician before undertaking any exercise program to make sure that you are physically safe to partake in these activities. A good cardiovascular workout is one that raises your pulse rate for extended periods. You should start with a slow pace, and increase the periods as your body adjusts to your routine. This will not only enable you to deal with stress in a healthier manner, but it will improve your overall health.

Anxiety is a feeling of unease. Everybody experiences it when faced with a stressful situation, for example before an exam or an interview, or during a worrying time such as illness. It is normal to feel anxious when facing something difficult or dangerous and mild anxiety can be a positive and useful experience.

However, for many people, anxiety interferes with normal life. Excessive anxiety is often associated with other psychiatric conditions, such as depression. Anxiety is considered abnormal when it is very prolonged or severe, it happens in the absence of a stressful event, or it is interfering with everyday activities such as going to work.

The physical symptoms of anxiety are caused by the brain sending messages to parts of the body to prepare for the "fight or flight" response. The heart, lungs and other parts of the body work faster. The brain also releases stress hormones, including adrenaline. Common indicators of excessive anxiety include:

1. Diarrhea
2. Dry mouth
3. Rapid Heart Beat
4. Insomnia
5. Irritability or Anger
6. Inability to concentrate
7. Fear of being "crazy"
8. Feeling unreal and not in control of your actions which is called depersonalization

Anxiety can be brought on in many ways. Obviously, the presence of stress in your life can make you have anxious thoughts. Many people who suffer from anxiety disorders occupy their minds with excessive worry. This can be worry about anything from health matters to job problems to world issues.

Certain drugs, both recreational and medicinal, can also lead to symptoms of anxiety due to either side effects or withdrawal from the drug. Such drugs include caffeine, alcohol, nicotine, cold remedies, and decongestants, bronchodilators for asthma, tricyclic antidepressants, cocaine, amphetamines, diet pills, ADHD medications, and thyroid medications.

A poor diet can also contribute to stress or anxiety -- for example, low levels of vitamin B12. Performance anxiety is related to specific situations, like taking a test or making a presentation in public. Post-traumatic stress disorder (PTSD) is a stress disorder that develops after a traumatic event like war, physical or sexual assault, or a natural disaster. Studies show that children that have been physically abused also can suffer from PTSD, and is often mis-diagnosed as some other disorder. We tend to relate Post-Traumatic stress disorder to veterans of wars, and this is simply not the case. It can occur from any traumatic incident be it a one time occurrence or an ongoing exposure to a traumatic experience.

In very rare cases, a tumor of the adrenal gland (pheochromocytoma) may be the cause of anxiety. This happens because of an overproduction of hormones and is responsible for the feelings and symptoms of anxiety.

While anxiety may seem a bit scary, what's even scarier is that excessive anxiety and stress can lead to depression. Suffering from depression can be a lifelong struggle as most well know, but the good news is that all of this is manageable!

**So, let's take a few little quizzes to see if you are suffering from too much stress, excessive anxiety, or depression.**

**Test Yourself**

This information has been compiled from many reliable sources and isn't meant to be a complete diagnostic tool in any way. These quizzes are simply guidelines to help you recognize any problems you might have and be able to effectively deal with those problems. Always seek professional medical attention from your family health care provider or a specialist for a proper diagnosis.

Because depression can be the most serious of our topics, let's start by seeing if you may be depressed. Keep in mind that everyone has their "blue" days. The factor that separates clinical depression from simple melancholy is that the symptoms occur over a longer period of time. They don't come and go, they stay around for awhile and can affect your life adversely.

Ask yourself the following questions. Answer yes if you've

been feeling this way consistently over a period of two weeks.

1. Do you find yourself constantly sad?

2. Are you un-motivated to do simple things like shower, clean up the house, or make dinner?

3. Do people tell you are overly irritable?

4. Do you have trouble concentrating?

5. Do you feel isolated from family and friends even when they are around you?

6. Have you lost interest in your favorite activities?

7. Do you feel hopeless, worthless, or guilty for no reason at all?

8. Are you always tired and have trouble sleeping?

9. Has your weight fluctuated significantly?

     If you can answer "Yes" to five or more of these questions, you could be suffering from clinical depression. It is important for you to seek out the help of a medical professional whether that be a psychologist, Psychiatrist or a therapist. I suggest you visit first with your family physician or regular Medical practitioner to rule out any physiological problems.

     If you feel you may be suffering from depression please do not be afraid, and mostly do not delay in seeking help. There are many medications out there that can help with depression.

Many people often try to deny their depression, but once they begin taking an anti-depressant, they have often said they couldn't believe what a difference that one pill a day made! It gives them freedom from the "black hole" they have fallen into and helped them to enjoy life again, so if you think you are depressed, ACT NOW! You deserve to have the best quality of life possible. Do not cheat yourself or your family!

This book is primarily about stress and anxiety, so let us see if you are overly stressed out. Ask yourself the following:

1.  Do you worry constantly and have periods of negative self-talk?

2.  Do you have a hard time concentrating?

3.  Do you get upset or mad and react to situations easily?

4.  Do you have neck pain or headaches often?

5.  Do you grind your teeth awake or in your sleep. (soreness is an indication of doing this in your sleep)

6.  Do you frequently feel overwhelmed, anxious or depressed?

7.  Do you feed your stress with excessive unhealthy eating or drinking habits, arguing, or avoiding yourself and life in other ways?

8.  Do you find that small pleasures fail to satisfy you as they had once been able too?

9.  Do you have incidents of rage or anger over minor problems?

If you can answer "Yes" to the majority of these questions, then you do have excessive stress in your life. The good news is that there is release and the fact that you bought this book will help you to learn many valuable ways to deal with that stress. Anxiety is the next area we will test.

1.  Do you often experience shortness of breath, rapid heart beat (palpitation) or the jitters (shaking) while at rest?

2.  Do you experience fear of losing control or feel you are going crazy?

3.  Does fear cause you to avoid social situations?

4.  Do certain objects cause you to experience fear?

5.  Do you fear that you will be in a place or situation from which you cannot escape?

6.  Do you have fear of leaving home?

7.  Do you have reoccurring thoughts or images that refuse to go away?

8.  Do you feel that you must perform certain activities repeatedly?

9.  Do you constantly relive an upsetting event from the past?
    If you have answered "Yes" to more than four of these questions it is a good indication that you suffer from an anxiety disorder.
    Suffering from depression, too much stress, or excessive

anxiety can endanger your overall health and it's time to take steps to overcome this – RIGHT NOW!

Stress and anxiety affects many factors in our body and not only in our mental state. Cancer and other deadly diseases are related to stress and anxiety because of the changes in the chemical composition in our body due to stress and anxiety.

You don't have to be a victim of stress and anxiety, it is all about discipline and having a proper schedule. Not taking in anything you cannot handle will be a lot of help. Learn your limitations and stick to them. Do not over exert yourself. Just try to go over the border an inch at a time.

You can lead a productive successful and fulfilling life and career without the need to endanger your health. If not, you are not only killing yourself, you are also sending your family and friends and all the people around you away.

Stress is a natural part of life. It can be both physical and mental and much of it can come from everyday pressures. Everyone handles stress differently, some better than others. Left unchecked, however, stress can cause physical, emotional, and behavioral disorders which can affect your health, vitality, and peace-of-mind, as well as personal and professional relationships.

## Panic Attacks

**As I have stated, stress and anxiety can lead to panic attacks. Speaking from experience, I can tell you that having a panic attack can be a serious situation. Let's take a look at that subject a little closer**

One of the unfortunate outcomes from suffering from excessive stress and anxiety is a physical reaction of your body to the situation. It's like your body is telling you that you need to rest for a moment. Except, when you're having a panic attack, it's anything but restful.

As I have written in a previous page, I have suffered from an anxiety attack. Fortunately I have not suffered from that since. I took it seriously and took immediate measures to ensure I had enabled myself to alleviate any and everything that could allow such an event.

The good news is that I wasn't dying – obviously! But you could not have told me that at the time. Many people are not as fortunate. It becomes a terrible journey for them in learning how their body reacts to excessive stress and anxiety. Many do take the correct actions, and do avoid stressors , and learn how to recognize that an attack might be coming on and how to control it. They are not always able to get hold of it completely and will occasionally fall into full-blown panic mode, but it's a lot better for them than it was. So even though you are not able to completely rid yourself of the problem any steps in the right direction will certainly help you to better cope.

So, let's look at the signs that indicate you might be having a panic attack. The following list gives tell-tale warning signs of an oncoming panic attack. (not exhaustive as it can vary from person to person).

•Palpitations

•A pounding heart, or an accelerated heart rate

•Sweating

•Trembling or shaking

•Shortness of breath

•A choking sensation
•Chest pain or discomfort

•Nausea or stomach cramps

•De-realization (a feeling of unreality)

•Fear of losing control or going crazy

• Fear of dying

•Numbness or a tingling sensation in your face and limbs
•Chills or hot flashes

You would be surprised at how many people go to the hospital emergency room completely sure that they're having a heart attack only to find out that it's a panic attack. They're that intense! I felt for sure that was what was happening to me.

Today with the current economic problems our country is experiencing hospitals are reporting all time highs of people seeking out the emergency room feeling as though they are experiencing a heart attack to find out after tests it had been Anxiety.

Our studies show a 420 percent increase in people going to emergency rooms for anxiety related disorders or thinking they are having a heart attack, only to find out it is an anxiety attack.
It's very difficult for your loved ones to imagine or even understand what you are going through when you have a panic attack. They may lose patience with you, tell you to "get over it", or think you're faking. It may help if you explain to them the following scenario.

You are standing in line at the grocery store. It's been a long wait but there's only one customer to go before you make it to the cashier. Wait, what was that?

An unpleasant feeling forms in your throat, your chest feels tighter, now a sudden shortness of breath, and what do you know—your heart skips a beat. "Please, God, not here."

You make a quick scan of the territory—is it threatening? Four unfriendly faces are behind you and one person is in front. Pins and needles seem to prick you through your left arm, you feel slightly dizzy, and then the explosion of fear as you dread the worst. You are about to have a panic attack.

There is no doubt in your mind now that this is going to be a big one. Okay, time for you to focus. You know how to deal with this – at least you hope you do! Start breathing deeply - in through the nose, out through the mouth.

Think relaxing thoughts, and again, while breathing in, think "Relax," and then breathe out. But it doesn't seem to be having any positive effect; in fact, just concentrating on breathing is making you feel self-conscious and more uptight.

Maybe if you just try to relax your muscles. Tense both shoulders, hold for 10 seconds, then release. Try it again. Nope, still no difference. The anxiety is getting worse and the very fact that you are out of coping techniques worsens your panic. If only you were surrounded by your family, or a close friend were beside you so you could feel more confident in dealing with this situation. Now, the adrenaline is really pumping through your system, your body is tingling with uncomfortable sensations, and now the dreaded feeling of losing complete control engulfs your emotions.

No one around you has any idea of the sheer terror you are experiencing. For them, it's just a regular day and another frustratingly slow line at the grocery store.
You realize you are out of options. It's time to run. You excuse

yourself from the line looking embarrassed as it is now your turn to pay. The cashier is looking bewildered as you leave your shopping behind and stroll towards the door.

There is no time for excuses—you need to be alone. You leave the store and get into your car to ride it out alone. You wonder whether or not this one was the big one. The one you fear will push you over the edge mentally and physically. Ten minutes later the panic subsides. It's only 11:00 in the morning, how in the world can you make it through the rest of your day?

If you suffer from panic or anxiety attacks, the above scenario probably sounds very familiar. It may have even induced feelings of anxiety and panic just reading it. I can remember all too well my experience.

The particular situations that trigger your panic and anxiety may differ. Maybe the bodily sensations are a little different. What's important to realize is that panic attacks are very real to the people who are having them and they should never be pushed off to the side.

This is an account recently told to me by an individual I had known when I owned a construction/consulting business in Atlanta. I will write this experience as best as I can recall and although it is not an exact quote, it is close enough to give you a good idea.
*I remember one evening at home when I was by myself watching one of my favorite television programs. I thought I was in a safe place. There was no obvious trigger and I felt completely relaxed. Out of nowhere, I began having symptoms of a panic attack. The four walls of my living room were closing in around me. I couldn't breathe and felt like I was dying. I stepped out on my front porch for some fresh air and began deep breathing exercises. The symptoms eventually went away, but it left me wondering why*

*exactly I had that attack. There was no obvious reason, no stressful*
*situation, and no indicator that a panic attack might be impending.*

That's the strange thing about panic. Sometimes your mind can play tricks on you. Even when you think you're in no danger of having a panic attack, your brain might be feeling differently. That's the scary part. The good part is that there are ways you can combat panic attacks and cope much better when you find yourself in that situation.

## Dealing With Panic Attacks

If you have panic attacks, it may help to comfort you that you are not alone! You're not even one in a million. In America, it is estimated that almost 5% of the population suffers from some form of anxiety disorder.

*I might add that this number is certainly increasing based on hospitals reporting that they have seen a rise in people coming to the emergency room thinking they were having heart attack, but later to find out it was anxiety. It would be interesting to know if local 911 centers have received an increase of calls as well.*

For some, it may be the infrequent panic attacks that only crop up in particular situations-like when having to speak in front of others, while, for other people, it can be so frequent and recurring that it inhibits them from leaving their home. Frequent panic attacks often develop into what medical physicians refer to as an "anxiety disorder."

There are many ways of coping with an anxiety disorder.

Some may not work for you, but others just might. It helps to know some of the most common coping techniques for dealing with panic attacks when they begin.

Your first step is to recognize when a panic attack is about to begin. When you have enough of them, you start to really pay attention to the tingling sensation, the shortness of breath, and the disconnection from the real life around you.

While my incident was not this severe many people I have talked to wonder what that disconnection is like. They have a hard time understanding it. Those that have ever experienced a panic attack this severe are all too familiar with it. They will tell you it is like you can look at a solid object and see that it is there. You know it's there, but a part of your mind doubts that it really is there. You may find yourself reaching out to touch that object just to be sure. You feel like you're not a part of the world around you. It's as if you are just a spectator in your own life with no control over anything around you.

So how do you start trying to combat your panic attacks? What if I told you the trick to ending panic and anxiety attacks is to want to have one. That sounds strange, even contradictory, doesn't it? But the "want" really does help push it away.

Does this mean that you should be able to bring on a panic attack at this very moment? Absolutely not! What it means is that when you are afraid of something – in this case a panic attack – it will more than likely appear and wreak havoc. When you stand up to the attack, your chances of fending it off are much greater.

If you resist a situation out of fear, the fear around that issue will persist. How do you stop resisting–you move directly into it, into the path of the anxiety, and by doing so it cannot persist. In essence what this means is that if you daily voluntarily seek to have a panic attack, you cannot have one. Try in this very moment to have a panic attack and I will guarantee you cannot. You may not realize it but you have always decided to panic. You make the choice by saying this is beyond my control whether it be consciously or sub-consciously.

Another way to appreciate this is to imagine having a panic attack as like standing on a cliff's edge. The anxiety seemingly pushes you closer to falling over the edge. To be rid of the fear you must metaphorically jump. You must jump off the cliff edge and into the anxiety and fear and all the things that you fear most. How do you jump? You jump by wanting to have a panic attack. You go about your day asking for anxiety and panic attacks to appear.

Your real safety is the fact that a panic attack will never harm you. That is a medical fact. You are safe, the sensations are wild but no harm will come to you. Your heart is racing but no harm will come to you. The jump becomes nothing more than a two foot drop! It's perfectly safe.

Anxiety causes an imbalance in your life whereby all of the mental worry creates a top-heavy sensation. All of your focus is moved from the center of your body to the head. Schools of meditation (which I do not necessarily agree with) often like to demonstrate an example of this top-heavy imbalance by showing how easily the body can lose its sense of center.

The key to overcoming panic attacks is to relax. That's easy to say but difficult to do. A good way to do this is to concentrate on your breathing making sure it is slow and steady. One of the first signs of a panic attack is difficulty breathing, and you may find yourself panting to catch a breath. When you focus on making those breaths even, your heart rate will slow down and the panic will subside.

Breathing more slowly and deeply has a calming effect. A good way to breathe easier is to let all the air out of your lungs. This forces your lungs to reach for a deeper breath next time. Continue to focus on your out-breath, letting all the air out of your lungs and soon you'll find your breathing is deeper and you feel calmer.

Ideally, you want to take the focus off the fact that you are having a panic attack. Try to press your feet, one at a time, into the ground. Feel how connected and rooted they are to the ground. An even better way is to lie down with your bottom near a wall. Place your feet against the wall (your knees are bent) and press your feet one at a time into the wall. If you can breathe in as you press your foot against the wall, and breathe out as you release it, it will be more effective. You should alternate between your feet. Do this for 10 - 15 minutes or until the panic subsides.

Use all of your senses to take full notice of what you see, hear, feel, and smell in your environment. This will help you to remain present. Panic is generally associated with remembering upsetting events from the past or anticipating something upsetting in the future. Anything that helps keep you focused in the present will be calming. Try holding a pet; looking around your room and noticing the colors, textures, and shapes; listening closely to the sounds you hear; call a friend; or smell the aromas that are near you. Many people strongly advocate aromatherapy to deal with panic and anxiety. Lavender can have an especially calming and soothing effect when you smell it. You can find essential oil of lavender at many stores. Keep it handy and take a sniff when you start feeling anxious. Try putting a few drops of lavender essence oil into some oil (olive or grape seed oil will do) and rub on your body. Keep a prepared mixture in a bottle or small container for when you need it. You can even prepare several bottles, with a small one to carry with you.

Other essential oils known to help panic and panic attacks are helichrysum, frankincense, and marjoram. Smell each of them, and use what smells best to you, or a combination of your favorite oils mixed in olive or grape seed oil. You want to prepare yourself before a panic attack happens. When you're not in a panicked state, make a list of the things that you're afraid will happen. Then write out calming things that tell you the opposite of your fears. Then you can repeat these things to yourself when the panic starts to come.

Prepare a list of things to do in case of panicked feelings, and it will be ready for you when you need it. Fill it with lots of soothing messages and ideas of calming things to do. Many find this to be a very helpful tool and will keep a small notebook they carry with them that has these positive affirmations in it. Panic can be a very scary thing to go through, especially if you're alone. Preparing for when the panic comes can really help reduce the panic, and even sometimes help to prevent it.

Another great tool to combating anxiety and stress is to use visualization.

## Calm Yourself With Visualization

The purpose of visualization is to enable you to quickly clear mental stress, tension, and anxious thinking. The visualization can be used when feeling stressed and is particularly useful when your mind is racing with fearful, anxious thoughts.

This visualization process, when practiced frequently, is very effective for eliminating deep-seated mental anxieties or intrusive thoughts. To gain maximum benefit, the exercise must be carried out for longer than 10 minutes at a time, as anything shorter will not bring noticeable results.

There is no right or wrong way to carry out the visualization. Be intuitive with it and do not feel you are unable to carry it out if you feel you are not very good at seeing mental imagery. As long as your attention is on the exercise, you will gain benefit.

It is best to do this exercise in a quiet place where you won't be disturbed, and then when you are more practiced you will be able to get the same positive results in a busier environment such as the workplace. You should notice a calming effect on your state of mind along with a sensation of mental release and relaxation.

Either sitting or standing, close your eyes and move your attention to your breathe. To become aware of your breathing, place one hand on your upper chest and one on your stomach. Take a breath and let your stomach swell forward as you breathe in and fall back gently as you breath out. Take the same depth of breath each time and try to get a steady rhythm going.

Your hand on your chest should have little or no movement. Again, try to take the same depth of breath each time you breathe in. This is called Diaphragmatic Breathing. When you feel comfortable with this technique, try to slow your breathing rate down by instituting a short pause after you have breathed out and before you breathe in again. Initially, it may feel as though you are not getting enough air in, but with regular practice this slower rate will soon start to feel comfortable.

It is often helpful to develop a cycle where you count to three when you breathe in, pause, and then count to three when you breathe out (or 2, or 4—whatever is comfortable for you). This will also help you focus on your breathing without any other thoughts coming into your mind. If you are aware of other thoughts entering your mind, just let them go and bring your attention back to counting and breathing.

Continue doing this for a few minutes. (If you practice this, you will begin to strengthen the Diaphragmatic Muscle, and it will start to work normally—leaving you with a nice relaxed feeling all the time.)

Move your attention to your feet. Try to feel your feet, really feel them. See if you can feel each toe. Picture the soles of your feet and picture roots growing slowly out through your feet and down into the ground. The roots are growing at a rapid pace and are reaching deep into the ground. You are now connected firmly to the ground and feel stable like a large Pine or Palm tree.

Keep this feeling of grounded safety for a few minutes. Once you have created a strong feeling or sense of being grounded like a tree, visualize a shape of bright light forming above you. A streak of lightning from the bright object hits the top of your head, and that ignites a arc of bright warm light descending slowly from your head all the way down your body, over your legs, and out past your toes.

As the band of light passes over you, feel it clearing your mind and thoughts. It is illuminating your mind and clearing any disturbing or stressful thoughts that you may have been thinking about. Repeat this image four or five times until you feel a sense of clearing and release from any anxious thinking.

In finishing, see yourself standing under a large bright waterfall. The water is beaming of light and bubbling with life. As you stand under the waterfall, you can feel the water run over every inch of your body, soothing you and causing within you a sense of deep calm.

Try to taste the water. Open your mouth and let it run into your mouth, refreshing you. Hear it as it bounces off the ground around you. The water is life itself and it is washing away stress and worry from your mind and body. After a moment, open your eyes.

Try to use all of your senses when carrying out the visualization. To make the pictures in your mind as real as possible, use your senses of touch, taste, and hearing. Feel the water trickle down your body; hear the sound it makes as it splashes over you.

The more realistic the imagined scenarios, the more benefit you will gain. Many people report very beneficial and soothing results from using these simple visualizations frequently. The mind is much like a muscle in that, in order to relax, it needs to regularly release what it is holding onto.

You can use any situation or location that will help calm you. I liken this to "finding your happy place". Maybe you feel relaxed in a swimming pool or on the beach. Imagine yourself there. Just make sure wherever you go in your mind is a place where you can be calm and rested.

By visualizing the different situations, you are allowing your mind to release. It is like sending a message to your brain that when you close your eyes and begin this process it is time for letting go of anything that it has been mentally holding onto, including anxious thinking.

In order to train your mind how to let go of the stress, it is important to practice this daily. With practice, you can learn to release all stress within minutes of starting the exercise. Your daily practice should take place before going to bed, as that will enable you to sleep more soundly.

Many people do not do these visualizations in the bedroom but some other room before going to bed. That way, when they enter the bedroom and close the door, they are leaving the mental stress and anxious thinking behind them. Just be sure you have the opportunity to totally concentrate on your mental images.

Visualization as a tool for dealing with mental stress is very effective. If such visualization is carried out properly, you can reach a deep feeling of inner calm. This technique probably will not work in helping to end an anxiety attack, but it can help that attack from beginning. It is a very powerful support tool for ridding yourself of general anxiety sensations.

With practice, you find you go days without having anxious thinking interrupt your life, and importantly, this significantly reduces the level of general anxiety you feel. Visualization is simply a tool you can use to overcome anxious thoughts and feelings.

Let's look at various ways that you can combat excessive stress – beginning with music.

## Using Music To Beat Stress

Listening to music does wonders to alleviate stress. Everyone has different tastes in music. We should listen to the music that makes us feel comfortable. Sitting down and forcing yourself to listen to relaxation music that you don't like may create stress, not alleviate it. Music is a significant mood-changer and reliever of stress, working on many levels at once.

The entire human energetic system is extremely influenced by sounds, the physical body responds specifically to certain tones and frequencies. Special consideration should be given to the positive effects of one actually playing or creating music themselves.

Among the first stress-fighting changes that take place when we hear a tune is an increase in deep breathing. The body's production of serotonin also accelerates. Serotonin is a hormone and neurotransmitter.

Playing music in the background while we are working, seemingly unaware of the music itself, has been found to reduce the stress of the workplace. That's why so many retail places play music while you shop – to take your mind off the high prices! Music was found to reduce heart rates and to promote higher body temperature - an indication of the onset of relaxation. Combining music with relaxation therapy was more effective than doing relaxation therapy alone.

Many experts suggest that it is the rhythm of the music or the beat that has the calming effect on us although we may not be conscious of it. They point out that when we were a baby in our mother's womb, we probably were influenced by the heart beat of our mother. We respond to the soothing music at later stages in life, perhaps associating it with the safe, relaxing, protective environment provided by our mother.

Music can be one of the most soothing or nerve wracking experiences available. Choosing what will work for any individual is difficult, most will choose something they 'like' instead of what might be beneficial.

In doing extensive research on what any given piece of music produces in the physiological response system many unexpected things were found. Many of the so-called meditation and relaxation recordings actually produced adverse EEG patterns, just as bad as Hard Rock and Heavy Metal.

The surprising thing was many selections of Celtic, Native American as well as various music containing loud drums or flute were extremely soothing. The most profound finding was any music performed live and even at moderately loud volumes even if it was somewhat discordant had a very beneficial response.

As I mentioned before, there is not a single music that is good for everyone. People have different tastes. It is important that you like the music being played. I recently downloaded a rest and relaxation mp3 to use while in my office to gauge its effects. I find that I can actually concentrate better and I am not very aware at all that it is playing. It has the sounds of the ocean in the background while beautiful piano music plays. It's very soothing. I intend to try one with the wind pipes as I love the sound of it.

One note here, it's probably not a good idea to play certain types of ballads or songs that remind you of a sad time in your life when you're trying to de-stress. The reason is obvious. You're trying to relax and wash away the anxious thoughts. The last thing that you need is for a sad song to bring back memories you don't need anyway.

**Here are some general guidelines to follow when using music to de-stress.**

- To wash away stress, try taking a 20-minute "sound bath." Put some relaxing music on your stereo, and then lie in a comfortable position on a couch or on the floor near the speakers. For a deeper experience, you can wear headphones to focus your attention and to avoid distraction.

- Choose music with a slow rhythm - slower than the natural heart beat which is about 72 beats per minute. Music that has repeating or cyclical pattern is found to be effective in most people. As the music plays, allow it to wash over you, rinsing off the stress from the day. Focus on your breathing, letting it deepen, slow and become regular. Concentrate on the silence between the notes in the music; this keeps you from analyzing the music and makes relaxation more complete.

- If you need stimulation after a day of work, go for a faster music rather than slow calming music. Turn up the volume and DANCE! It doesn't matter if you can actually dance or not. Just move along with the music and do what feels good. You'll be shocked at the release you can feel! When going gets tough, go for a music you are familiar with - such as a childhood favorite or favorite oldies. Familiarity often breeds calmness.

- Take walks with your favorite music playing on a portable player. Inhale and exhale in tune with the music. Let the music take you. This is a great stress reliever by combining exercise (brisk walk), imagery and music.

- Listening to the sounds of nature, such as ocean waves or the tranquility of a deep forest, can reduce stress. Try taking a 15- to 20-minute walk if you're near the seashore or a quiet patch of woods. If not, you can buy tapes of these sounds in many music stores.

I have just recently tried "relaxation" music and it has proved to have very beneficial and very calming effects for me – you should try it!

There's another great relaxation technique I actually used in basic training in the Air Force to help me fall asleep not being used to hitting the sack at 9:30pm: self-hypnosis.

## Self-Hypnosis For Stress

There are many books, and audios both on and off-line that you can purchase to help you learn this technique. It is rather simple.

You first need to find a quiet place where you can fully relax and listen to your inner voice. You should not try to make something happen. Let your mind listen and relax. A large part of achieving that hypnotic state is to allow it to happen naturally. Also, don't watch for certain signs or signals that you might be in a hypnotic state. I can guarantee that if you look for these signs, you won't be able to fully relax and gain the benefits of self-hypnotic experience.

There are lots of different ways to experience hypnosis. No two people will have exactly the same experience. In one respect, though, everyone has the same experience: the hypnotic state is always pleasant! There are no "bad trips" in hypnosis. Keep in mind that self-hypnosis is a skill, and that you will continue to get better at it and, as you do, it becomes ever more powerful.

It's a good idea to set up a schedule of practice, allowing yourself anywhere between 10 and 30 minutes, depending on how busy you are and how much time you have to spend at it. Practice during the best part of your day if you can and at a time when you are least likely to be disturbed by others. Most people find it best to practice lying down, in a comfortable position, with as few distractions as possible. If you are bothered by noise while you practice you can try to mask out the noise with some other source of sound.

You can try stereo music in the background, or white noise if you like. For those of you who do not have a white noise generator, try tuning a radio receiver between the stations. The static you get when you do that is similar to white noise. You will need a cheap or older FM receiver without a noise suppressor. Sometimes AM tuners can be used for this. This should just be in the background and not too loud to be distracting.

The basic divisions of a hypnotic induction are *relaxation,deepening, suggestion application,*and *termination.*

## 1. Relaxation
Your first job in the hypnotic induction is to slow your system down and get yourself relaxed. But don't try to force your mind to relax (whatever that means)! If you get yourself physically relaxed, your mind will follow.

Relaxation – really deep relaxation – is an ability that most people have either lost or never developed. Some people can do it quite easily though. They just let go of their tensions and let every part of their body become limp and relaxed. If you are one of these people, begin your self-hypnosis practice by getting nicely relaxed. Take your time. This is not something you want to rush.

The time involved for the relaxation phase of your self-hypnosis induction can vary from half an hour to just a few seconds. It is an important part of the induction and should not be slighted. As you get better and your skill increases you will recognize deeply relaxed states, and you will be able to achieve them in a surprisingly short time. But as a beginner, take your time. It will be time well spent.

A very popular method of deep relaxation is the Jacobson Progressive Relaxation procedure. This involves tensing each of the major muscle groups of your body (foot and lower leg on each side, upper leg and hip, abdomen, etc.). Tense the muscle group for a few seconds, then let go.

## 2. Deepening Procedures

Once you have completed the relaxation phase of your self-hypnosis induction procedure, you can begin to deepen the relaxed state. At some time between the deep relaxation and the deepening procedures you will move into a hypnotic state. You probably won't know it, especially as a beginner, but it will happen sooner or later. One of the first hurdles a beginner must get over is the compulsion to "watch for it." That is, you will keep waiting for hypnosis to happen, for some change in your awareness or the way you feel that will say to you, "You're hypnotized."

Watching for hypnosis will definitely get in your way if you don't get it out of your mind. Going into a hypnotic state is, in this respect, similar to going to sleep. If you try to catch yourself going to sleep – if you try to be aware of the precise instant in which you actually go to sleep – you are much less likely to go to sleep. "Watching" keeps you awake. In this same way you will not know when you go into a hypnotic state (but that *won't* be because you lost consciousness – you won't). Later, after you have been practicing regularly for a few weeks or a month or two, you'll be much more familiar with yourself and how it feels to be hypnotized.

Does it take everyone weeks or even months to get into a good hypnotic state? Absolutely not. Some people have tremendous results the very first time they try it. Others might practice for several days, noticing nothing, then *out of the blue* they have one of those great induction sessions in which they know something stupendously good happened. But if you happen to not be one of these people, don't worry about it. Just keep at it. Practice, Practice, Practice!

**3.** One of the most popular deepening procedures is the **count-down technique**.

Hollywood also likes this one. That is why you see it in so many movies. That and the swinging watch.

To use the count-down technique you simply start counting downward from, say, 20 (or 100, or whatever). Adjust the countdown number to whatever feels right to you after you have practiced a few times. Imagine that you are drifting deeper with each count. Other images and thoughts will probably intrude themselves as you count. That is natural. Just gently brush them aside, continuing with your counting.

The speed with which you count down should be natural; not too fast, not too slow. For most people this means counting at a rate of about one count for each two or three seconds. Do it at a rate that feels comfortable and relaxed to you. Some people like to tie the count with their breathing. As they drift deeper their breathing slows down, so their counting also slows down.

Don't count out loud, just *think* your way down the count. You want to avoid as much physical involvement and movement as possible.

## 4. Suggestion Application in self-hypnosis

Once you have reached the end of your deepening procedure you are ready to apply suggestions.

What you have done during the relaxation and deepening procedures is increase your suggestibility. That is, you have opened up your subconscious mind at least a little bit to receive your suggestions. This works because of the particular, and peculiar, characteristics of the subconscious part of your mind.

The most common and easiest way to apply suggestions is to have them worked out ahead of time, properly prepared and worded, and memorized. It should not be too difficult to remember them because they should be rather short and you are the one who composed them. If you have them ready and remembered, you can simply think your way through them at this point.

Dialogue, or more properly monologue, is also okay. You just talk ("think" to keep your effort to a minimum) to yourself about what it is you want to do, be, become, whatever. Don't say "you." You are thinking to yourself, so use the first person personal pronoun "I." Some suggestions can be succinctly stated in a somewhat more formal sort of way, like, "I am eating less and becoming more slender every day."

Elaborated suggestions are generally wordier and more of an ad lib: "Food is becoming less important to me every day and I am filling my time with more important and meaningful pursuits than eating. It is getting easier and easier to pass up desserts and other fattening foods" and so on.

Generally speaking, the most effective kind of suggestion is image suggestion. Image suggestions usually do not use language at all. You can liken this to seeing yourself in a calm, relaxed state while in the middle of a chaotic situation. Actually see yourself in your mind's eye. Although people sometimes see immediate results from their suggestions, it is more likely to take a little time for them to kick in. So don't be impatient. On the other hand, if you have not begun to see some results within, say, a couple of weeks, you need to change your suggestions.

## 5. Termination

Once you have finished applying suggestions you are through with your induction and you can terminate your session. You could just open your eyes, get up and go about your business, but that is not a good idea. You should formally identify the end of every session. By doing this you provide a clear boundary between the hypnotic state and your ordinary conscious awareness. A clear termination also prevents your self-hypnosis practice session from turning into a nap. If you want to take a nap, take a nap. But don't do it in a way that sleeping becomes associated with self-hypnosis practice. If you are practicing at bedtime and don't care if you go on to sleep, that is okay. But still draw the line in your mind to indicate the end of your self-hypnosis session. To terminate the session, think to yourself that you are going to be fully awake and alert after you count up to, say, three. "One, I'm beginning to come out of it, moving toward a waking state. Two, I'm becoming more alert, getting ready to wake up. Three, I'm completely awake." Something like that. Self-hypnosis can work wonders when it is practiced on a regular basis. You'd be amazingly surprised at the level of relaxation you can get to. Let's move on to stress management techniques in general. This chapter is critical and helpful.

## Stress Management

As I said before, stress is a part of life. There's no getting away from it. In fact, some stress is good stress. You may not believe that, but sometimes stress can motivate us to do things we may not normally do in a relaxed state. Stress can make us brave enough to go forward when normally we might hesitate. I often say I work better under stress. There is much truth for me in that statement. It does seem that I can accomplish enormous amounts of work when under stress.

We have to be resilient in order to effectively cope with stress and help it enhance our life instead of <u>control </u>it. How do you get strong and resilient? By learning how to take control of your stress and make it work for you instead of against you.
Recognizing stress symptoms can be a positive influence in that we are compelled to take action – and the sooner the better. It's

not always easy to discern why you have the stress in each situation but some of the more common events that trigger those emotions are the death of a loved one, the birth of a child, a job promotion, or a new relationship. We experience stress as we readjust our lives. Your body is asking for your help when you feel these stress symptoms.

I am going to give you many suggestions in this chapter. Not all of them will work for you, but I am willing to bet that some of them will.

There are three major approaches to manage stress. The first is the **action-oriented** approach. In this method, the problems that cause stress are identified and necessary changes are made for a stress free life.

The next approach is **emotionally oriented** and in it, the person overcomes stress by giving a different color to the experience that caused stress. The situation, which causes stress, is seen humorously or from a different angle.

I especially advocate this approach to stress management. Sometimes if you don't laugh at a situation, you will – uncontrollably. That's no solution. So learn to see the humor instead of the doom.

The third way is **acceptance-oriented** approach. This approach focuses on surviving the stress caused due to some problem in the past. The first stress management tip is to understand the root cause of your stress.

**1. Understand the root cause**. No one understands your problem better than you do. A few minutes spent to recognize your true feelings can completely change the situation. During this process, identify what triggered the stress. If someone close to your heart is nearby share it with the person. If you are overstressed and feel you are going to collapse, take a deep breath and count till ten. This pumps extra oxygen into your system and rejuvenates the entire body.

When under severe stress stop and employ one of your relaxation techniques for a moment and pull out of the current situation for a little while. Stand up from your current position and walk. Stretch yourself. Soon you will find that the stress has lessened. This is because you have relaxed now and relaxation is the best medicine for stress. Smiling is yet another way of stress management. If you are at the work place, just stand up and smile at your colleague in the far corner. You will see a change in your mood. It is important to learn and to practice your relaxation techniques.

You can also invent your own stress management tips. The basic idea is to identify the cause of stress and to pull out from it for a moment and then deal with it. Taking a short walk and looking at objects in nature is another stress reliever. Drinking a glass of water or playing small games are simple stress management techniques. The whole idea is change the focus of attention and when you return to the problem, it does not look as monstrous as it felt before.

**Here are the rest of the quick steps you can take toward relieving stress:**

**2. Don't just sit there. Move!** From my own experience and from many other experts motion creates emotion. You might notice that when you are idle, it's easier to become depressed. Your heart rate slows down, less oxygen travels to your brain, and you are slumped somewhere in a chair blocking air from reaching your lungs. I challenge you right now, regardless of how you are feeling, to get up and walk around at a fast tempo. Maybe you might want to go to an empty room and jump up and down a little bit.

It may sound silly but the results speak for themselves. Try it now for a few minutes. It works like magic. Exercise can be a great stress buster. People with anxiety disorders might worry that aerobic exercise could bring on a panic attack. After all, when you exercise, your heart rate goes up, you begin to sweat, and your breathing becomes heavier.

**3.  Don't panic – it's not an attack!** Tell yourself this over and over while you're exercising. Realize that there's a big difference between the physical side of exercise and what happens when you exercise.

**4.  Smell the roses.** How do you smell the roses? How about investing some money to go on that one trip you've been dreaming about? Visit a country with lots of interesting places to jolt your imagination and spur your creativity. You need to detach from your daily activities and venture a little bit. I am very guilty of never taking time for myself. I am suppose to be retired now, and as many know, I actually work more hours than before, but it is on things I thoroughly enjoy and get great satisfaction from.

**5.  Help others cope with their problems.** It is very therapeutic when you engross yourself in helping others. You will be surprised how many people's problems are worse than those you may be facing. You can offer others assistance in countless ways. Don't curl up in your bed and let depression and stress take hold of you. Be careful here. From my experience most people once they see that there is a solution to their problem will immediately feel so much joy they want to heal others instead of first ensuring they have taken care of themselves. Get out and help somebody. Again, be careful. Don't get caught up in other people's problems in an attempt to forget about your own.

I do not know to get advice and many times as it turns out to just vent. I always take time out for these type of calls no matter what I am involved with. I must admit there are times that I catch myself worrying about the ones who call me. I am careful and have a healthy way of keeping myself detached from others problems. This can be a deadly pitfall for counselors or you if not careful. Some tend to internalize other peoples problems. I know of a few who have actually left the counseling field as a result of this. If you see this to be the case for you stop as it will give you more stress than you already have. This is certainly a great thing, helping others, but be careful not to allow it to add stress therefore being counter productive. You will learn to tell them that you just can't deal with it right now and to call back later. Sometimes, they get upset, but more often than not, they understand. But you will learn not to get too upset about their reactions. You have to learn to place yourself first in this area.

**6. Laugh a little.** By now you've heard that laughter is a good internal medicine. It relieves tension and loosens the muscles. It causes blood to flow to the heart and brain. More importantly, laughter releases a chemical (endorphin) that rids the body of pains. Every day, researchers discover new benefits of laughter. Let me ask you this question: "Can you use a good dose of belly-shaking laughter every now and then?" Of course you can. What are you waiting for? Go a comedy club or rent some funny movies.

**7.  Wear your knees out.** If there were one sustainable remedy I could offer you when the going gets tough, it would be prayer. Many people, depending on their faith, might call it meditation. It doesn't matter to me what you call it, as long as you have it, and you use it. Now you have a few quick fixes for times that you feel overwhelmed with stress. Need more?

**More Stress Management**

**8.  Make stress your friend.** Acknowledge that stress is good and make stress your friend! Based on the body's natural "fight or flight" response that burst of energy will enhance your performance at the right moment. I've yet to see a top sportsman totally relaxed before a big competition. Use stress wisely to push yourself that little bit harder when it counts most.

**9.  Stress is contagious.** What I mean by this is that negative people can be a huge stressor. Negativity breeds stress and some people know how to do nothing but complain. Now you can look at this in one of two ways. First, they see you as a positive, upbeat person and hope that you can bring them back "up". If that's not it, then they're just a negative person and can't feel better about themselves unless those around them are negative as well. Don't get caught up in their downing behavior. Recognize that these kinds of people have their own stress and then limit your contact with them. You can try to play stress doctor and teach them how to better manage their stress, but be aware that this may contribute more to your own stress, so tread lightly.

**10.   Copy good stress managers**. When people around are losing their head, what keeps them calm? What are they doing differently? What is their attitude? What language do they use? Are they trained and experienced? Figure it out from afar or sit them down for a chat. Learn from the best stress managers and copy what they do.

**11.   Use heavy breathing.** You can trick your body into relaxing by using heavy breathing. Breathe in slowly for a count of 7 then breathe out for a count of 11. Repeat the 7-11 breathing until your heart rate slows down, your sweaty palms dry off and things start to feel more normal.

**12.   Stop stressful trains of thought.** It is possible to tangle yourself up in a stress knot all by yourself. "If this happens, then that might happen and then we're all up the creek!" Most of these things never happen, so why waste all that energy worrying needlessly?

Give stressful thoughts the red light and stop them in their tracks. Okay so it might go wrong – how likely is that and what can you do to prevent it? Learn a simple prayer I picked up while working with people with addictions. The serenity prayer. I actually have it framed in my office.

God grant me the serenity to accept the things I cannot change; courage to change the things I can;and wisdom to know the difference.

**13.  Know your stress hot spots and trigger points**.
Presentations, interviews, meetings, giving difficult feedback, tight deadlines....... My heart rate is cranking up just writing these down! Make your own list of stress trigger points or hot spots. Be specific. Is it only presentations to a certain audience that get you worked up? Does one project cause more stress than another? Did you drink too much coffee?

Knowing what causes your stress is powerful information, as you can take action to make it less stressful. Do you need to learn some new skills? Do you need extra resources? Do you need to switch to decaffeinated coffee?

**14.  Eat, drink, sleep and be happy!**Lack of sleep, poor diet and no exercise wreaks havoc on our body and mind. Kind of obvious, but worth mentioning as it's often ignored as a stress management technique. Listen to your mother and don't burn the candle at both ends!

Avoid using artificial means to deal with your stress. That means don't automatically pour a glass of wine when you think you're getting stressed out and don't light up a cigarette. In actuality, alcohol, nicotine, caffeine, and drugs can make the problem worse. A better idea is to practice the relaxation techniques I have suggested. Then, once you're relaxed, you can have that glass of wine if you want.

**15.  Go outside and enjoy Mother Nature.** A little sunshine and activity can have amazing ramifications on your stress level and will enhance your entire outlook towards life. Your improved attitude will have a positive effect on everyone in your family and/ or circle of friends; things which seem overwhelming will soon become trivial matters, causing you to wonder what the predicament was. Not only will you be less stressed, you will be healthier, happier, and more energetic; ready to face whatever obstacles come your way.

**16. Give yourself permission to be a 'kid' again.** What did you enjoy when you were a child? Draw; paint; be creative. Play with Playdough, dance, or read. Play music, allow yourself freedom to express yourself without worry that you're not keeping with the image of who you are 'supposed' to be. Just relax and enjoy yourself. We all have a little child in us and it's a good idea to allow expression of the child within from time to time.

I can attest to the benefits of this myself. There are many times I simply throw my hands up and say that's it. I crank up my stereo to my favorite music and jam out tight in my office. Sometimes I might even dance around a bit. Does anyone know. I could care less, its fun and I feel better after a session of just letting my hair down. Try it. Who cares, not as many folks are watching you as we like to believe and if they are perhaps you may cause them to break loose and try it as well.

**17. Don't set unrealistic goals for yourself**. Many of us set ourselves up for defeat simply by setting unrealistic goals for ourselves. For example, if you are dieting, realize you cannot lose 45 pounds in one to two months. Not in any healthy way that is. Maybe you are trying to reach a goal of obtaining a particular job position; whatever your goal is allow sufficient time to reach your goals and realize that you may experience occasional setbacks.

If you reach your goal without any delays, you will be even happier with yourself for arriving sooner than you had planned, but just do not expect it. A good practice is to not expect anything; expectations and reality are often two entirely different things.

**18.   Learn it is OK to say 'no' to people occasionally.** Many of us feel we have to say 'yes' to everyone, every time we are asked for help and feel that we must respond in a positive fashion. I am very guilty of this myself and if not careful we end up over loading ourselves and not fulfilling promises, and then people get the wrong idea and we have just added more stress to our lives.

Remember, you cannot be all things to all people. You must first meet your own needs before you can truly give others what they need while at the same time keeping yourself happy.

You do not have to do everything your family, friends, and others ask. Of course you can help others, but first make sure you have done what is necessary to take care of yourself. Make time for yourself, your number one priority; once your own needs are met you will find you have more time for others. And you may find more pleasure in helping others when you do not feel that you must always put others needs before your own. Do not fret I am not finished yet! There are so many great ways to combat stress and anxiety. You deserve to get all the information you can. After all, that's really why you're reading this book, isn't it? Here are some more stress busters.

**More Ways To Stop Stress In Its Tracks**

**19.   Many people swear by this one. Yell!** That's right, scream at the top of your lungs – as loud as you can. While this may not be feasible in your home, it works great when you're in your car with the windows rolled up. Let out a loud yelp from deep down inside. It's liberating!

**20.   Sing.** As I said in the previous chapter, music can be extremely beneficial when getting rid of stress. Think how much better you can feel when you belt out you favorite lyrics at the top of your lungs! Who cares if you can't carry a tune? You're doing this for you!

**Take up a new hobby like wood work or knitting.**

**21.   Don't worry about being good at it.** It's the process that's beneficial. Sitting still while performing repetitive movements is calming and stabilizing for many people. It can be time to collect your thoughts.

**22.   Start a garden.** Even apartment dwellers can do this. Inside in pots, pots on the patio, pots, a small spot in your yard. There is a little work to setting it up.

Tending to plants, fruits, vegetables, flowers and watching them grow, bloom, or yield food is rewarding. Avid gardeners say working a garden is the best way to control stress and worry. An added benefit is the creation of a more beautiful, restful environment.

**23.   Play with a dog or cat.** Experts say pet owners have longer lives and fewer stress symptoms than non-pet owners. Playing with your pet provides good vibrations for you and for the pet! It's a form of social interaction with no pressure to meet anyone's expectations!

**24.   Look at the stars and the moon.** It can be a very humbling experience to lay on a blanket with your hands behind your head and gaze up into the night sky. It's more than humbling; it's downright beautiful and relaxing!

When I had property in Florida on North Captiva Island there were many nights I would go out and lay on the beach at night all alone. Look up at the awesome sky, away from all the city lights. Spectacular it was. Coupled with the sound of the ocean I cannot remember a more relaxed time as the times spent doing that. All my troubles seemed to melt away as I experienced the clear and beautiful sky and realizing the awesomeness of its creator. Try it sometimes if you have not. Just grab an old blanket and take off outside. Share it with someone , but I encourage you to try it alone sometimes. You will understand the enjoyment I got from it. If you have never done this you have really missed out on a lot.

**25. Treat yourself to some comfort food**. But be careful or overeating could become your big stressor. Enjoy in moderation and make yourself feel better.

I love ice cream. That would be my comfort food. There are many southern dishes I greatly enjoy but ice cream is my weakness. I can grab a half gallon of cheese cake flavored ice cream and be completely at peace. I have to be real careful with ice cream. I do not even keep it in the house. When I feel I need it I go out and buy it, and do so in small portions. If I kept it at home I have learned from experience I would simply eat it all up, and fast. We know what ice cream can do, and does to me if not careful.

**26. Swing.** Remember the feeling of sitting inside that little piece of leather on the playground as you sway back and forth. Do that! If you don't have a swing in your yard, go to a playground and remember to pump your legs back and forth to see how high you can go. It's liberating! Who cares what people think. They are just jealous that they do not have the courage to have fun, to act like a child once again.

**27. Take a candle lit bubble bath.** Even us guys out there can benefit from a warm bath bathed in the soft glow of candlelight.

My daughters mother loved this and often used aromatherapy candles. I soon appreciated the benefits of it. Lay your head back, feel the bubbles and the warm water, and let your stress go right down the drain when you pull the plug!

I have given you twenty seven ways to de-stress You can come up with your own. The key is to find something that makes you feel better when you are overwhelmed. When you do find the right thing for you practice it often. You will see how great the benefits are.

## Sometimes You Have To Learn To Just Say No!

One huge problem people who are overly stressed out have is the ability to say "No" when they need to. It could be a simple as someone asking you to run an errand for them or someone asking you to fill in and work for them. Whatever the case may be there is no reason why you have to say "Yes" to everyone. In fact, there are often many times when you should turn them down. If you find yourself agreeing to do things when you really don't want to, you're a people pleaser. Many will say this isn't a bad trait to have, but right or wrong I find it to be a bad trait and it can certainly be a huge stressor. Sure we should be helpful, but in my opinion people pleaser's are those of low self esteem. That is another issue and a controversial one so lets not go there as we are here to relieve stress, not generate it. So let's just assume it is acceptable.

People pleaser's think of other people's needs before their own. They worry about what other people want, think, or need, and spend a lot of time doing things for others. They rarely do things for themselves, and feel guilty when they do. It's hard being a people pleaser.

People pleaser's hold back from saying what they really think or from asking for what they want if they think someone will be upset with them for it. Yet they often spend time with people who don't consider their needs at all. In fact, people pleaser's often feel driven to make insensitive or unhappy people feel better, even at the detriment to themselves.

Constantly trying to please other people is draining and many people pleaser's feel anxious, worried, unhappy, and tired a lot of the time. They may not understand why no one does anything for them, when they do so much for others, but they often won't ask for what they need.

This is the trap many fall into. They find themselves always agreeing to do for others, but when they need those same people to help them out, they are curiously occupied.

A people pleaser may believe that if they ask someone for help and that person agrees, that person would be giving out of obligation, not because they really wanted to. The thinking goes - if they really wanted to help, they would have offered without my asking.

This line of thinking happens because people pleaser's themselves feel obliged to help and do not always do things because they want to. Sadly, people pleaser's have been taught that their worth depends on doing things for other people.

It's painful being a people pleaser. People pleaser's are not only very sensitive to other people's feelings, and often take things personally, but they also rarely focus on themselves. When they do take a moment for themselves, they feel selfish, indulgent, and guilty which is why they are often on the go, rushing to get things done. Because people pleaser's accomplish so much and are easy to get along with, they are often the first to be asked to do things - they are extremely vulnerable to be being taken advantage of.

People pleaser's were most likely raised in homes where their needs and feelings were not valued, respected, or considered important. They were often expected as children to respond to or to take care of other people's needs. They may have been silenced,neglected, or otherwise abused, thus learning that their feelings and needs were not important.

In many cultures, girls are raised to be people pleaser's, and to think of others' needs first, and to neglect their own. Many women have at least some degree of people pleasing in them. Men who identified with their mothers often do as well.

People pleaser's focus is mostly on others and away from themselves. They often feel empty, or don't know how they feel, what they think, or what they want for themselves. But it's possible to change this pattern and to feel better about yourself.

Many have managed to learn how to break out of this cycle. You can do the same thing if you see yourself in the above description. You want to know how? It's easier than you think! First, practice saying **NO**. This is a very important word! Say it as often as you can, just to hear the word come out of your mouth. Say it out loud when you are alone. Practice phrases with NO in them, such as, "No, I can't do that" or "No, I don't want to go there". Try it for simple things first, and then build your way up to harder situations. Stop saying **YES** all the time. Try to pause or take a breath before responding to someone's request. You may want to answer requests with "I need to think about it first, I'll get back to you" or "Let me check my schedule and call you back". Use any phrase that you feel comfortable with that gives you time before you automatically respond with YES.

Take small breaks, even if you feel guilty. You won't always feel guilty, but most likely in the beginning you will. Remember that your mental health is well worth the aggravation you may have to take from others. What's important is you. When you are healthy, those around you will be healthy!

Figure out what gives you pleasure. For example, you may like reading magazines, watching videos, going to a park, or listening to music. Give yourself permission to do those things and then enjoy them.

Ask someone to help you with something. I know this is a hard one but you can do it! After all, everyone else is asking YOU for favors, why shouldn't YOU ask THEM? Just be tolerant if they turn you down. Just because you have always told them "Yes" doesn't mean they always have to tell you "Yes".

Check in with how you feel and what you are thinking. It's important to be aware of these things; they're part of who you are. And then try saying what you feel and think more often. Just remember to have a little decorum in certain situations.
Many people pleaser's believe that nobody will like them if they stop doing things for other people. If someone stops liking you because you don't do what they ask, then you're being used by them and probably don't want them as a friend anyway.

People will like you for who you are and not simply for what you do. You deserve to take time for yourself, to say NO, and to take care of yourself without feeling guilty. It's within your reach to change. One small step at a time!

I think most people would be in agreement when I make this next statement. McDonald's had it right when they coined – You Deserve A Break Today!

## Time To Take a Break -Ya Think?

So often, we know inside ourselves that we need a break. That break might be a full-fledged vacation or a weekend getaway. Either way, getting out of the daily grind can be amazingly liberating and a huge way to get rid of stress and anxiety. Above all else I am an expert on this particular subject. I am ever so guilty of this – not taking a break.

Unfortunately, many people think they can't take the time to get away. This is dangerous thinking. Get out and get away! How many times have you continued working, knowing that you are not giving one hundred percent to the task at hand? How many times have you read or written the same sentence over and over again, as your mind keeps wandering and thinking about other things? How often have you wanted to take a break from the family or kids but feared the consequences of doing so? It's time for a break!

Why do we not allow ourselves the time to take a 'time out'? Perhaps we feel like we don't deserve it or that there's just too much to be done. There are many genuine reasons for needing to complete jobs and tasks; however we may also on occasion have 'hidden agendas' as to why we cannot stop for a break. Why?

It could be ego. Some people simply enjoy boasting about, 'how late they had to work in order to complete a project' or 'how much effort they invested in order to complete the job so quickly'. This type of person is often looking to impress others with their efforts, thereby increasing their ego in the process.

Maybe you think you just can't take the time off. "I can't stop; I just have to get this finished". Does this sound familiar? "I can't stop because the job has to be finished, WHY? So I can move straight on to the next thing, and the next, and the next etc..." This person will find that there is always something that has to be done, which will constantly prevent them from taking a break.

Maybe you just feel like you need to be needed. A mother managing the household, kids and other chores may feel as if her household will collapse if she were to put her feet up or take a weekend off! A manager may feel the company would fold or the employees just will not perform well in his or her absence. By not taking a break they can keep convincing themselves that their role is crucial and things would collapse without them.. This may indeed be true, but is still not a good enough reason to prevent one from having a rest!

Get rid of that thinking! You can get some amazing benefits just by taking a little time for yourself! Allowing your mind and/or body to rest can help re-focus your attention, sharpen your wits and increase motivation. In addition, taking time out helps to relieve stress, can aid the recovery of tired muscles and also promotes the discovery that there is more to life than just work.

Many athletes will tell you that an important part of their training routine is rest. Muscles need time to repair.. Remember that your brain is a type of muscle as well. It needs time to rest and recuperate in order to perform at its best. By giving your brain time off, you'll be able to better concentrate and give tasks you once found difficult your full attention. They'll be easier, trust me!

So you've decided that a break is in order. Good for you! A break can be anything from a 10-minute relaxation session to a trip around the world, and anything in-between. I think a break should be something that takes your mind off from a preoccupation with the everyday tedium of life.

So depending on the time you wish to avail towards relaxing you may enjoy reading, watching a movie, cooking, playing with the kids, riding a motorbike or driving, exercising or doing sports, traveling or simply sleeping!

While you are taking this rest, above all, allow yourself the time to do it and don't feel guilty.
You will gain so very much by this time off, so enjoy the time you are giving yourself.

Life will go on without you and contrary to what your mind might be telling you, everyone will survive – even when you're not there! Let everything go and concentrate on YOU for once instead of everyone around you!

If you're feeling tired, de-motivated or just in need of a rest, don't be a martyr or look negatively at this. You may actually find that in reality, allowing yourself a break will actually help you ultimately become more efficient and effective in every part of your life. Plus you'll get the badly needed recharging of your "batteries" that you need and sorely deserve!

Work can probably be one of the most stressful places to be. You might think that none of these techniques can help you when you're around your co-workers. You couldn't be more wrong.

## Relaxing At Work

Coffee breaks aren't the only times when you can take a moment for yourself. In reality coffee and smoking can add loads to your stress. The chemicals in these products are proven to add to it. Many will disagree especially smokers. While it may be true in the case of smokers that a smoke calms them down scientific studies say otherwise. I have to tell you the truth I am a smoker that would argue it. We all have our vices many simply do not have the courage or are too egotistical to admit it.

Some of the suggestions I have given you in this book can certainly be practiced at work, but, unfortunately, others cannot. Here's a tried and true method to help you relax at work.

First and foremost, find a place to sit. Sit up straight with your back against the back of your chair, your feet flat on the floor, and your hands resting lightly on your thighs. If possible, close your eyes. You may do the exercise without closing your eyes, but closing your eyes will help you relax a bit more. Do not clench your eyes shut. Let your eyelids fall naturally. Breathe in slowly through your nose, counting to 7. Hold the breath for a count of 7. Breathe out slowly, counting to seven. Repeat.

This exercise is performed by tensing and holding a set of muscles for a count of 7, and then relaxing the set of muscles for a count of 7.

When you tense each muscle set, do it as hard as you can without hurting yourself. When you release the hold, be as relaxed as possible.

Begin by tensing your feet. Do this by pulling your feet off the floor and your toes toward you while keeping your heels on the floor. Hold for a slow count of five. Release the hold. Let your feet fall gently back. Feel the relaxation. Think about how it feels compared to when you tensed the muscles. Relax for a count of five.

Next tense your thigh muscles as hard as you can. Hold for a count of 5. Relax the muscles and count to 5. Tighten your abdominal muscles and hold for a count of 5. Relax the muscles for a count of 5. Be sure you are continuing to sit up straight.

Tense your arm and hand muscles by squeezing your hands into fists as hard as you can. Hold for a count of 7. Relax the muscles completely for a count of 7. Tighten your upper back by pushing your shoulders back as if you are trying to touch your shoulder blades together. Hold for a count of 7. Relax for a count of 7. Tense your shoulders by raising them toward your ears as if shrugging and holding for a count of 7. Relax for a count of 7.

Tighten your neck first by gently moving your head back (as if looking at the ceiling) and holding for 7. Relax for 7. Then gently drop your head forward and hold for 7. Relax for a count of 7. Tighten your face muscles. First open your mouth wide and hold for 7. Relax for 7. Then raise your eye brows up high and hold for 7. Relax for 7. Finally clench your eyes tightly shut and hold for 7. Relax (with eyes gently closed) for 7.

Finish the exercise with breathing. Breathe in slowly through your nose, counting to 7. Hold the breath for a count of 7. Breathe out slowly, counting to seven. Repeat 4 times. And that's it! Perform this exercise whenever you need to relax, whether it's on a plane or in a car or anyplace else you may be sitting. Because this exercise may be very relaxing, it should not be performed while driving.

Over time, if performed regularly, this exercise will help you recognize tension in your body. You will be able to relax muscles at any time rather than performing the entire exercise. Perform at least twice a day for long-term results.

You may develop your own longer relaxation exercise by adding more muscle groups. Pinpoint your own areas of tension then tense and relax these areas in the same way.

Maximize the relaxation benefits of this exercise by visualizing a peaceful scene at the end of the exercise. Visualize a scene - a place where you feel relaxed - in detail for at least 5 minutes. Remember this happy place? Go there and enjoy it, and RELAX!

## Symptoms Quick List

### You should know the symptoms of an anxiety attack

Many experience anxiety attacks or panic attacks including children. Not all anxiety attacks lead a person to an anxiety disorder. Researchers put a great deal in understanding the root cause of anxiety attacks and the symptoms of mild anxiety attacks.

**Fear** is the major symptom of an anxiety attack. It is not the normal form of fear that we are accustom to dealing with, but some creeping sensation that once you feel you can hardly stop thinking about it. Before the fear reaches your conscious level, it slinks your subconscious mind. In other words, the fear is actually submerged and it influences you from a deeper level of understanding.

**Heart Palpitation** You find your heart is racing and it is impossible to get it under control. The symptoms of an anxiety attack become apparent due to the adrenaline secretion in the body. Although adrenaline secretion is good for the body in that it prepares us for 'flight or fight'. However, excessive secretion of adrenaline may lead to real complications.

**Dizziness and feeling light headed** You feel detachment from reality. Since nothing seems real and everything seems to have changed, you feel again a sense of anxiety of foreign presence, leading you to
potentially experience more panic attacks over time.

**Intense Feeling of Danger** Individuals with panic attack experience an intense feeling of danger. Many researchers believe that an individual with panic attacks may have developed an idea of perceived danger to such extent that he/she may consider themselves weak, while their surroundings are powerful and it is a threatening place to survive. The individual feels that that he/she is going to be harmed or worst die. This only worsens the attack or attacks.

**Feeling of Helplessness or Hopelessness** An individual having a panic attack finds himself helpless which intensifies the problem to greater extent. Since an intense feeling of helplessness or hopelessness at one hand and an urge to survive from perceived danger from the other, the individual experiences unusual conflict which leads him to experience more acute shortness of breath. This can slowly shift the condition from mild to severe.

## Pharmaceutical Medications for Anxiety/Stress

Certain drugs that are commonly prescribed for stress and anxiety may be habit forming and those are appropriately marked. In most cases as it should be these that are habit forming are used for short term relief allowing a long term medication time to build up in the body. You will want to take care in using these habit forming drugs due to the fact many doctors have simply over prescribed them. It is your health and you have to be proactive. So please be aware and educate yourself on all medications prescribed. Do not be afraid to ask question or get a second opinion if you are not satisfied with the care you are receiving.

There are many types of medication on the market to combat anxiety/stress. One can find it difficult to know which course of action to take. It is always best to seek professional care and to allow them to formulate a specific treatment plan for you that is designed for your specific needs and one that considers your specific stressor, and triggers.

You should always be proactive in your treatment and be

aware of the various drugs available. These medications listed are only available by prescription, but you should be aware of what you are putting in your body. Never be afraid to ask your health care provider if a particular medication may be better for you or safer than the one he or she may prescribe.

There are three main types of drugs available when it comes to anxiety or stress. Anti-Anxiety drugs claim to combat anxiety, but anti-depressants have grown in popularity over the last decade and have become the most common treatment.

You will find that there are three forms of anti-depressants as follows:

1.  **Selective Serotonin Reuptake Inhibitors**

2.  **(SSRIs)Tricyclic Anti-Depressants Monoamine Oxidase**

3.  **Inhibitors (MAOIs) SSRIs** have become the most popular of the three. They tend to have less negative side effects than many of the older drugs and can be used in a generalized manner when dealing with various causes of your anxiety. They are used in treating the following but not limited only to these forms.

1.  Social Anxiety
2.  Obsessive Compulsive Disorder (OCD)
3.  Panic Disorder

The neurotransmitter Serotonin is responsible for stabilizing arousal, controlling aggressive impulses, stabilizing your mood, and lessons anxiety. When there is insufficient serotonin there is a heightened chance of experiencing high levels of stress or anxiety.

SSRIs prevent the neurotransmitter serotonin from being reabsorbed therefore making available more for the body to utilize.

**These are Brand names of the common SSRIs**

- Prozac
- Celexa
- Paxil
- Zoloft

When a patient is not responsive to SSRIs Tricyclic Anti-Depressants are prescribed. These medications are older than the SSRIs and work similarly. **Trycyclic Anti-Depressants** also prevent serotonin from being reabsorbed. In addition it also prevents the neurotransmitter norepinephrine from being reabsorbed as well. They also have much higher incidents of negative side effects. Dizziness, constipation, urinary problems, and vision problems may be a few of the negative effects to name a few.

**Brand names for popular Trycyclic Anti-Depressants**

- Elavil
- Tofranil
- Anafranil

The third are **Monoamine Inhibitors** (MAOIs). Monoamine Oxidase is an enzyme the body produces that breaks down the neurotransmitters that combat anxiety. MAOIs block this enzyme. MAOIs are prone to have very negative effects at times with certain foods and can lead to a stroke hence the reason they are prescribed with great caution and usually when the other forms have failed to work.

## Brand Names for Monoamine Oxidase (MAOIs)

- Nardil
- Parnte
- Marplan

## Benzodiazepines are commonly prescribed for anxiety (Habit Forming)

Always provide your health care provider with accurate information. If you have ever had any form of addiction or addiction related problems your provider needs to know. Benzodiazepines may not be wise for a person that has had prior addiction problems.

**Benzodiazepines** were at one time the main treatment for anxiety and related disorders. Benzodiazepines are a tranquilizer. They work fast in alleviating stress and anxiety where SSRIs and Trycyclic, and MAOIs need time to build up in your system. Benzodiazepines work on the neurotransmitter gamma-aminobutyric (GABA). It slows brain activity reducing racing thoughts and calming the nerves.

They are very beneficial to stop a panic attack or to help lessen the severity of an attack as they work very fast. They can, and are in many cases used in conjunction with one of the other medications to give the patient immediate relief should an attack occur. The preferred method of treatment would be to allow the SSRIs or one of the other medications to begin to work in your system and then tapper you off the benzodiazepine. Most

Physicians do not allow the patient to continue benzodiazepines for extended periods, but in some cases it is warranted and should be closely monitored.

Benzodiazepines work well in treating phobias and generalized anxiety. Again, much care should be given when taking benzodiazepines. Always include in your medical history any problems with addiction. You do not want to add to your anxiety by developing a drug problem.

**Brand names for a few benzodiazepines**

- Xanax
- Ativan
- Valium

**An alternative to benzodiazepines is Buspar**

It works by stimulating serotonin receptor sites on the nerve cells that need the serotonin in order to alleviate anxiety. This medication reduces nervousness, and helps reduce fear that accompanies anxiety disorders. It does not have the sedative effect like benzodiazepines. Buspar can potentially have negative side effects as is with any medication. Bear in mind that you may not experience any of the reported effects. It is policy that any effects have to be reported. With that in mind possible side effects can be, but not limited to nausea, insomnia, headache, and excitement.

Buspar has its own possible withdrawal effects such as

irritability. It is not as likely to become addictive nor are patients as likely to abuse buspar as with benzodiazepines. Again, exercise caution.

I will drive this point in the ground. Always include any addiction or related problems in your medical history. Another point I will always drive home is that you should be proactive in your treatment.

## Natural Alternatives

Always speak with your medical provider before taking any form of medication especially if you have already been prescribed a medication. Depending upon the type of medication you may be prescribed there are "over the counter" medications that may have adverse effects. Always consult with your health care provider before adding any other medications, natural, over the counter or prescribed. Many people see different doctors for various reasons so be sure to keep them informed as to what medications you are taking. Keep a journal if need be. It is ever so important that they know, and they will not know unless you tell them. Not a safe area to make assumptions.

Listed are some of the most frequently recommended natural remedies.

You can easily look these up in your favorite search engine if the links fail to work or if you have purchased this book in paperback. We can not control the workability of links to other sites as they make changes frequently. Try the links first and then if they fail use your search engine.

**Valerian Root (*Valeriana Officinalis*)**Promotes relaxation to relieve occasional anxiety and panic. Learn more about Valerian Root

**Passion Flower (*Passiflora Incarnata*)**Non-drowsy natural sedative that relieves nervousness, nervous tension and occasional anxiety. Learn more about Passion Flower

**Winter Cherry**
**(*Withania Somnifera*)** Relieves anxiety and other occasional emotional stress responses. Learn more about Winter Cherry

**Rhodiola Rosea(*Rhodiola Rosea*)** Widely recognized for its broad spectrum of action to relieve occasional anxiety and support the body during time of stress. Learn more about Rhodiola Rosea

**St. Johns Wort (*Hypericum Perforatum*)**Clinically shown to be a natural reuptake inhibitor. May help to promote a healthy neurotransmitter balance. Learn more about St. John's Wort

**5-HTP(*5-Hydroxytryptophan*)**Derived from plant sources. 5-HTP acts as a precursor to Serotonin, a neurotransmitter that regulates mood balance. Learn more about 5-HTP

# Conclusion

If you have learned nothing from reading this book, I hope you realize and understand that there is no way to completely eliminate stress from your life. What you can do is to learn how to make that stress work for you.

Stress management isn't as difficult as it might actually seem. However, I can't emphasize this next point enough. If you think you have too much stress in your life, it may be helpful to talk with your doctor, spiritual advisor, or local mental health association. Because reactions to stress can be a factor in depression, anxiety and other disorders. They may suggest that you visit with a psychiatrist, psychologist, social worker, or other qualified counselor.

I am coming out soon with a book that deals with depression. To get on a list to be notified simply email me at EarthOne.Books@gmail.com Also visit our website www.earthone-books.com

I do not profess to have all the answers. I am a Christian Counselor and have been well educated in cognitive studies, and addiction counseling. I choose this path as many do who enter the counseling field. You have those licensed under the criteria that the State regulates and the States also offer Christian Counselors the option to practice under the prescribed guidelines set aside for them. This is the avenue I chose. I have obtained my Doctorate and have a significant amount of experience in the field.

You may also want to look into time management tools in order to get rid of some of your stressors. When we feel like we don't have enough time to do the things that need to be done, that creates more stress and can lead to anxiety which, you don't want to have!

Stress management tips are simple cost effective methods to effectively check stress. They can be practiced anywhere and at anytime.

If you feel you are in need of help, do not hesitate. The cause of your stress might be for no reason at all. But it might be physical in its roots. Someone else might be able to solve it easily. Understand your limitations and it can relieve stress to a large extent.

Stress is a normal part of life. In small quantities, stress is good, it can motivate you and help you be more productive. However, too much stress, or a strong response to stress, is harmful. It can set you up for general poor health as well as specific physical or psychological illnesses like infection, heart disease, or depression. Persistent and unrelenting stress often leads to anxiety and unhealthy behaviors like overeating and abuse of alcohol or drugs.
Just like causes of stress differ from person to person, what relieves stress is not the same for everyone. In general, however, making certain lifestyle changes as well as finding healthy, enjoyable ways to cope with stress helps most people. I hope that I've given you some great ways of dealing with the stress that we all feel!

Above all, remember that you are in no way alone in this battle. There are hundreds of thousands of people out there who feel overwhelmed and nearly completely out of control. That's why I wrote this book in a fashion that I hope is understandable to anyone that chooses to read it so you can find peace within yourself and realize that we're all on this big blue and green marble for a reason. You are too!

Enjoy it and live life to its fullest. And when you feel yourself stressed out or beset with a panic attack, relax, breathe through it, and know that there are many, many people who know exactly how you feel.


VIVA EN AMOR!
Mark Taylor

*Mark Taylor*

Dr. Mark Taylor